None of the Above…

The Power & Pitfalls of Worship

None of the Above…

The Power & Pitfalls of Worship

By

Tommy Shavers

Cover Design: Noah Johnson

Published by

Commit 2 Publishing
Orlando, FL 32878

ISBN 13: 9780989941747

ISBN 10: 0989941744

Printed in the United States of America

Table of Contents

Created for Worship

Inspiring, mesmerizing, charismatic, powerful, beautiful, attractive, famous—these are just a few of the many words used for individuals of great status and social power in our society. Often societal leaders in many respects, these individuals are usually leaders as spiritual, sports, political, celebrity, and business figures. Yet, along with such high and admirable depiction comes behavioral descriptions like moral failures, abusive behaviors, objectification of humanity, and god-like complexes. These are the sad but true statements about the same individuals we admire and look up to as leaders or individuals who all have tremendous amounts of social status.

What in the world is happening to these people? Why in the world are we as a society still in awe of them time and time again, despite such behaviors? Although this is primarily a book written to help Christian believers

7

understand that the greatest attack on the church lies within its own walls, it is also a book to create awareness about the great challenge to humanity from a spiritual perspective. I want to clarify something from the start because it will be critical to how you as a reader process the information in this book.

This book is not speaking to any specific situation that has occurred in the lives of individuals, churches, or religious groups in general. I say this because it will be tempting as you read to make direct inferences to situations you have knowledge of or have heard about that seem to fit the explanations in this book. Don't do it. While it's possible for situations to have similarities in how things develop and evolve, each set of circumstances are totally different and have their own set of unique variables.

What you will read should not be used to justify, attack, question, or criticize the behaviors of others. The information found within the pages of this book should be used to create awareness and understanding on how to recognize, address, and potentially prevent the ever-growing crisis of ungodly behavior in Godly communities from those with power and others who are heavily influenced by their power.

Chapter 1: Getting the Story Straight

Understanding the Beginning

In the beginning, the origin of everything created us. Let me give better clarity to that statement. In [our] beginning, the creator of everything decided to make us also. I clarify this because it is important that we read into the statement what I believe is the accurate intention of the statement. Often when we read or have been told about Moses' story of human origins in Genesis, we picture this being [God] who is all alone is this empty existence and needs someone or something to share a relationship with. Enter humanity to the rescue! To make a long story short (which is usually impossible for me), we imagine God making us because he needs someone to express his love to and thus become complete.

We have been told many times that the story is about us—humans. So from the beginning, we are taught spiritually to filter or process our understanding of life through this lens that tells us we have this high place of need in the eyes of God. We are told of a love story of God pursuing man with a desire of wooing them back to him, back into a relationship with him.

Although not intentional, this view of the beginning creates a premise that sets the stage, from my perspective, for some of the behavioral challenges we are now facing in society as well as within the spiritual community. The premise is that 1) everything revolves around us (humanity) as the center of attention and that 2) God needs a relationship with us, which also implies that God needs us. When we look at human life through this lens, we create a mental model that makes us more than we are and God less than he is. We create this love-story image of God pursuing a relationship with humanity, while humanity is playing hard to get.

What we are not aware of is that this puts God 1) horizontally on the same plain as humanity and 2) in the trail position—as in, being in pursuit. He is placed on equal footing and in the follower position in relation to mankind. This mental picture thus gives us as humanity permission to define ourselves subconsciously almost as equals to God— or at least, just as important in the story as he is.

God Created Man

Back to our beginning; we are told we were *created by* God, in the *image of* God. Created by God gives us the picture of the *origin of power* itself creating something by his power. When God creates, it is never a horizontal or equal relationship, but a descending or superior-to-inferior relationship. I know this may seem like no-brainer stuff to you, but trust me; it is important to state from a foundational standpoint. The accurate picture of God tells us that he is not in the trail position running toward us, but that he is looking down on us from above. He is in the superior position; the position of power. In essence, humanity was made to look up (and bow down). We were made to be in relationship with our creator who made us and who is above us in the superior position. Humanity, therefore, was made to look up or be in submission to power because we were made to look up to and be in submission to God. God is the all-powerful origin of power itself.

"To whom will you compare me? Or who is my equal?" says the Holy One. *Lift up your eyes and look to the heavens. Who created all these? ~Isaiah 40:25–26*

As a public speaking instructor, I often stress how important eye contact is in engaging and connecting with your audience. However, for some students, eye contact was always a challenge—not because they were shy or nervous, but because of what the gesture meant to them in their culture. For some students, looking someone in the eye, especially individuals of higher social status, was a sign of disrespect. To look down when speaking to someone conveyed awareness and a valuing of that individual's comparatively higher status. This gesture was often shown to parents, teachers, the elderly, males, and other individuals recognized for their social status. I believe such cultures are on the right track.

Being made in the image of God is where things get tricky. In creating humanity in his image, the aspect of us that reflects God is power. God gave humans the power to make and the power to rule over. The power to make is a tremendous power; however, it has sometimes been explained inaccurately. It has often been explained as humanity being creators or co-creators with God. Here again, we see this idea of man being co-participants or

14

equals with God. God did not actually give us the power to create, but the power to make.

Some may think this is just a play on words. Words create meaning, and meanings influence behavior, so please never underestimate the importance of understanding words. To explain the difference between *create* and *make* is simple. *Create* implies making something from nothing, while *to make* implies making something from something else. Creating is being brought into existence; making is being made from existence. As humans we never create; we always make. We take from what God has already brought into material existence, and we make something of it.

To rule over conveys that we as humans are in a superior position to something or someone below us. This means that something or somebody is looking up to us in the dynamics of relationship. So humanity was made with a hierarchal element to its societal living. When Adam and Eve *made* another human being through childbirth, we are told that their son was made in the image and likeness of his maker, Adam. So we see in the parental relationship that there was an established hierarchy of power as well. The one who *made* the child was greater in power than the child

15

that was made. Thus when God created man, he created man from his power, and he created man to have power. Having the capacity to have power is one thing, but having the capacity to infer power to another is something totally different. Having the power to give others power declares the greater power of the power-giver over the power-receiver.

God created man relationally to do three things: 1) *to look down* in the superior position upon what they had power to reign over, 2) *to look straight* in the eye-to-eye or equal position at those who were created by God in the same capacity as man, and 3) *to look up* in the inferior position to what had power to reign over them. We read in the fourth chapter of Genesis that men began to call on the name of the Lord; in other words, men began to look up. This statement speaks to the relationship that humanity very early on innately began to understand and express that they were made in a worship relationship with God.

While Paul was waiting for them in Athens, he was greatly distressed to see that the city was full of idols. So he reasoned in the synagogue with both Jews and God-fearing Greeks, as well as in the marketplace day by day with those who happened to be there. A group of Epicurean and Stoic philosophers began to debate with him. Some of them asked, "What is this babbler trying to say?" Others remarked, "He seems to be advocating foreign gods."...

Paul then stood up in the meeting of the Areopagus and said: "People of Athens! I see that in every way you are very religious. For as I walked around and looked carefully at your objects of worship, I even found an altar with this inscription: TO AN UNKNOWN GOD. So you are ignorant of the very thing you worship—and this is what I am going to proclaim to you..." ~Acts 17:16–23

The degree of status and power from the superior position in the relationship determines the degree of influence on the behavior of the inferior position. Another way of describing this is what I call the eye-level status analogy. Where the eyes look tells us the status and power of what we look upon. Figuratively speaking, the higher up we look, the greater the intensity we feel pulling us submissively toward that which is exalted above us. The lower we look, the less intense the submissive pull upward, and the more intense the dominion pull downward. The position of the object and the intensity of the pull are driven by status and power.

When the power and status of the superior position are high and the power and status of the inferior position are significantly low in comparison, this creates the atmosphere for a worship relationship. An exchange relationship of admiration and love from one who is low in power or status toward another who has great power and status is the recipe for a worship relationship. Worship therefore is the intense admiration, love, and devotion shown to someone (or something) because of who they are (status) or what they are able to do (power).

Where the eyes look tells us if we are in the worshiper or object of worship position. Worship always comes from an inferior, eyes-looking-up position. It has been said that the reason for worship is found in love. While I agree that love plays a significant part in worship, love is not the only part. The greatest command is to love God with everything. Love turning into worship depends on where the eyes are looking. The command to love God is a looking up type of love, and God's command to love others is a looking straight across type of love. Only one of these creates worship, as worship is not a peer level type of love but an inferior-to-superior level type of love.

Why Do We Worship?

We worship because we are awed by what our objects of worship can do that we can't do—run fast, jump high, throw far, sing well, etc.—or by the fact that they're doing what we don't have to opportunity to do, thus displaying a status hierarchy that they are higher than us. Worship is a connection that allows us to feel and experience the pleasure of intense admiration toward something or someone of significance. Worship has its origins in what we know today as admiration. To admire simply means to feel fondly or positively about something or someone. Current research has shown that admiration has an effect of our behavior. In fact, studies have shown that admiration influences how we behave by regulating social hierarchies. In other words, when we admire someone, we are influenced to behave in such a way that supports them being in a high place of status and power. So if we admire someone, we can become inclined to defer to the individual of our admiration.

I remember hearing an interview done by a former White House Press Secretary about his book that painted the former president and his administration in a negative light. When asked why he waited until after the fact to say things he never expressed while being a part of the administration, the former Press Secretary expressed his initial admiration for the President and his belief in him and his commitment to change Washington politics. He went on to say that he gave the President the benefit of the doubt and that he had put his trust in the President and his team. It was only when he was no longer a part of the White House administration that he was able to take a step back away from it all. He mentioned that it was only after doing so that he was able to see things differently. Now I am not writing to express agreement or disagreement about the issues the former Secretary addresses; what caught my attention was the way he describes how admiration influenced his behavior.

When asked why his words of disapproval are now coming out in the form of a book, his response in so many words was because while in the presence of the Presidential culture, his admiration had him seeing things a certain way and behaving in a certain manner. However, once outside that culture, his views on things began to change. This is the perfect example of how admiration can influence behavior. I consider myself to be a pretty independent thinker (many who know me would say that's an understatement). However, I confess that many times while in the presence of individuals I admire or individuals of high status, I believe I have been under some spell of admiration.

I often found myself in agreement with whatever was being said or shared in the moment. If I didn't agree, I tried to find a way to make sense of what was being said because I gave them the benefit of the doubt that they were accurate and I was not. It would only be when I would leave their presence and go home and talk to my wife that the trance or spell would wear off, and I was able to see things objectively again. I found myself saying things like, "What was I thinking; I don't agree with that." However, when I would be in their presence again (on the phone or in person) my mind would be changed again, and I would be in agreement with them.

This was when I began to realize that high admiration for the powerful could possibly have a real impact on one's ability to be objective. This is what makes cults works, what creates loyal followers or supporters of certain individuals, and what allows the ideologies of some to be championed over others. My doctoral study research would confirm my beliefs that those with status and power can influence the thoughts and behaviors of those that admire them greatly. This high level of admiration combined with the great disparity of status and power leads to what we know to be worship.

Look at how humanity was made with the inclination to worship something or someone higher than themselves—and the things we are willing to do for those we worship and place in such high regard. Moses was not gone on the mountain with God long before the people felt they needed to make a god because they needed an object to worship. They needed something greater than themselves to serve, honor, follow, obey, worship. We are drawn in our hearts toward worshiping and idolizing things and beings that are perceived as greater than ourselves. Christian leaders would tear their robes in distain toward the people when they would attempt to idolize them or make them objects of worship. The people even wanted to take Jesus by force and make him king. They were looking for not only someone to follow but someone to worship.

A Worship Atmosphere

We talk a lot in church circles about an atmosphere of worship. The conversations about an atmosphere for worship are usually focused on how can we cultivate or manipulate our external surroundings to enhance the experience people feel when they are in our "worship" services. This could be anything and everything from the style of music, audio visual tactics, lighting, song choices, etc. While I believe there is evidence in scripture for excellence and quality when it comes to musical praise and worship, an atmosphere of worship doesn't start here. As mentioned earlier, an atmosphere for worship starts when there is a recognized and embraced disparity of status and power between God and man in a social relationship.

Singing can only be considered worship if those singing are engaged in a true worship relationship with God.

For there to be worship, there has to be a relationship—more specifically, a relationship between something or someone who is in the exalted position and someone who is in the lowered or humble position. Worship is a neutral social experience. There is no moral compass that guides the heart when it comes to worship. If the individual in the lower position of status and power is drawn emotionally to something or someone of much higher status or power, then he or she will become inclined to worship. This is why God in his commandments to the Israelite nation in Exodus 20 focused the first two commandments on proper worship; if they didn't get commandments one and two correct, they were not going to be willing or able to follow the rest of the commands, because you follow wholeheartedly who or what you worship.

"I am the LORD your God, who brought you out of Egypt, out of the land of slavery. You shall have no other gods before me." ~Exodus 20:2–3

God said to have no other God but him. The commandment implies that we can develop an atmosphere of worship with something or someone other than God (we'll touch on this more later).

"You shall not make for yourself an image in the form of anything in heaven above or on the earth beneath or in the waters below. You shall not bow down to them or worship them; for I, the LORD your God, am a jealous God…" ~Exodus 20:4–5

He then tells the people in his second command more specifics about the first command. He states not only will you not have another God, you will not have anything, whether from his creation or from your own making, that you will establish a worship relationship with. The fact that God has to state this should tell us something. The first thing it should tell us is that we were created by God to worship. We know this because we know that we were created into a high/low relationship and are wired to be pulled toward that which is greater than ourselves. Secondly, it should tell us that for whatever reason, worshiping something or someone other than God is a real possibility. As God tells us in the second commandment, there are beings and things he created that are so much greater than us that we can even become inclined to worship them. He also says that we are capable of even manufacturing ourselves, from our own doing, an atmosphere of worship that is not directed toward God.

Who or what we worship determines who we are, what we do, and how we live. The ultimate power will have our ultimate worship and thus our ultimate obedience. God starts with these first two commands because if he hadn't, then the other remaining commandments as well as the additional laws and regulations he gave the people would've been useless. The power they acknowledged as greatest would be the God they would have as their God. The God they would have would be whom they would worship. Whom they worship would be whose regulations and laws they would follow. Keep in mind that these people had been slaves for 400 years in a place that did not follow or worship God. The better way of saying this is that they spent 400 years following and worshiping everything else besides their God. Therefore, the first two commandments dealt with worship because God was correctly reestablishing the leader/follower or creator/created relationship in the lives of his people. This would be the only way they could truly follow him—if they truly worshiped him and him alone. These insights are the premise of where this book will go on this topic. We will look in more detail at how we were wired to worship and the practical impact that has on who or what we worship today in our society, both inside and outside of the church walls.

Today we continue to be a world of worshipers of the created more than worshipers of the creator. The devil's goals are twofold: 1) to remove worshipers from God and 2) to claim worshipers for himself. Satan tried to get Jesus to worship him. Remember the exchange offer he proposed to Jesus—to give him everything on the condition that he would worship him. Jesus, being the son of God, was being tempted to receive power and dominion over what his father had created. Now even as a minister with an advanced degree in biblical studies, I can confidently say that I cannot fully understand how Satan could make such an offer other than the fact that he was lying.

He was attempting to sell something he didn't really own. Satan's proposal was that everything would worship Jesus if Jesus worshiped him. He was attempting to remove God from his rightful place and place himself on the throne. If he attempted to get Jesus to worship him and failed, it shouldn't surprise us that his goal is also to get us as humans to not worship God. Satan would much rather we worship him—or worship what he is placing in our world as objects of worship as alternatives to God himself.

The same proposal Satan offered to Jesus, he is offering to humanity, and we are eating it up like hotcakes! He is offering us everything—most importantly, the opportunity to become objects of worship. What would make such an offer seem so appealing? Well to Jesus, it wasn't appealing at all because he already had what Satan was trying to sell him. In fact, he had much more; he had everything because he is the Son of God. A regular person, on the other hand, sees Satan's offer as very appealing. Since the beginning, he has attempted to entice and intrigue us with the possibility of what it must be like to be God.

As a kid who was raised by a single mom who did farming and fieldwork for a living, I didn't have a lot growing up. I recall at times seeing friends with name-brand clothes and the latest toys and video games, wondering what it must be like to live in their worlds every day. I was intrigued, even envious at times. I wanted what they had because I wanted to experience how it felt having more. This was what Satan put before Eve in the garden—the opportunity to experience what it's like to be like God, to have more! The dangers of such a proposition are numerous; however, the opportunity for many throughout the centuries has been one that seemed just too enticing to pass up. What if you could be like God; would you do it? What cost would you be willing to pay for such an experience? Jesus said no to Satan because he was already the complete likeness of God. Man, on the other hand, throughout the years has said to Satan, "I'm intrigued; tell me more."

The Hidden Cost

As with any scam or agenda-driven deal, there is always a hidden or undisclosed cost. I once called a well-known flooring company to have them come in and place wood floors in our home. They were offering something like 30 or 40 percent off the entire job. We thought that was a great deal, but unfortunately, when they came to do the job, both I and my wife were too preoccupied with other things to really overlook the contract the way we normally would. They did the work, we paid the cost, and they left. When it came time to do my taxes, I was looking at the receipt and realized that there was not an individual breakdown of the work, its total cost, and then the percentage discount. I called the company to request a detailed receipt, only to get rejected and told that they didn't provide details on their individual costs, only on overall costs. How are people supposed to know if they are actually getting a discount if they are not able to know what the original cost was from the beginning? Satan does not want us to know the actual cost of worshiping created things. All he wants us to know is that it feels good and that we have the *power* to do so.

The actual costs of worshiping created things are astounding. The first cost is the more we worship people in power, money, lifestyles, celebrities, athletes, pastors, etc., the less we worship God. Secondly, the more we experience worshiping created things or being worshiped by created things, the more we desire it and are drawn to it. Thirdly, we begin to value and admire God less as we value and admire other things more. Lastly, the more we experience being worshiped, the more god-like we are becoming. The problem, however, is having god-like powers with just a human capacity to handle them. The ultimate plan of Satan is to create a power status here on earth wherein people learn to follow, admire, and worship the power within others (as opposed to God). His end goal was and still is to replace God in the lives of people so that we worship and follow the power and status of unrighteousness and not righteousness.

Chapter 4: The god-like Complex

As humans, we were made to worship and not to be worshiped. As a result, people in all walks of life are being corrupted and destroyed by the power and worship-like treatment they are receiving from others. This is playing a huge role in moral and ethical failings in the lives of many because they are being treated like gods without the capacity to handle god-like treatment. God can handle being worshiped and is worthy of it because he is greater and higher than all; there is none above him. But man was not created with the capacity to handle being worshiped because we are not gods; we are not greater or higher than our fellow men.

I heard a podcast on biblical humility from D. A. Horton, Executive Director of Reach Records, that caught my attention. During the podcast he made the statement that our praise does not add value to God. This statement made sense to me because we can't lift God up any higher than he already is. In Luke 2:14, we read of the angels singing praise to God, saying, "Glory to God in the highest." Their praise of God in song points out that 1)

God deserves recognition worthy of praise because of who he is (glory), and 2) God is already in the highest position possible and can't get any higher as a result of their praise of him. In fact, it is because he is in the highest place that they are singing praises, proclaiming his glory.

Although our praise can't lift God up any higher than he is, it can lift up man higher than he should be. Praise lifts up. With God, praise merely acknowledges that he is already lifted up; however, with man, it actually lifts us up. Praise does add value to man. In Matthew 23 Jesus gives a masterful threefold discourse on the pitfall of human praise. He was *preaching* to the crowds while *teaching* his disciples and *rebuking* the scribes and Pharisees. Jesus tells the crowd and his disciples that their spiritual leaders had become corrupted by their high places and the praise they received from their spiritual status among the people. They loved their high places, their rock-star-like treatment from the people, and the acknowledgement that they were greater than those around them. This is the true definition of being proud. *To exalt* is to place high or lift up, and to be proud is to appear above others; thus being proud is the result of being exalted. Whether exalted by others or self, humans have the potential of becoming proud.

As a result, Jesus points out in a rebuking fashion that the lives of the spiritual leaders had become more influenced by their own uplifted status rather than by the uplifted status of God. They had become proud in their hearts. They were living for the pursuit of praise instead of the pursuit of righteousness. While their outside lives always looked worthy of praise, their inside lives were earning them wrath and condemnation from God. Sadly, we see this issue in growing numbers among our spiritual leaders today as well.

The lives of these types of spiritual leaders revolve around how their actions can result in more praise and exaltation from their followers. As a result they become blind to how their actions and behaviors are being seen by God; God is removed from the picture. Exalted people who fall in love with the praise they receive will eventually remove God from the picture completely. When God is removed from the picture, these exalted individuals will ultimately develop what I refer to as the god-like complex.

The Complex

The god-like complex is a mentality people develop when they believe they can do and have anything they desire because of their status, power, and idolizing treatment they receive from followers or admirers. This belief isn't just arrogance; in fact, it is often a real belief that has developed from the god-like treatment they receive from those around them and society in general. With God, whatever he does is right. His people are required to submit to his actions and choices, not vice versa. When a person is placed is a position of high status and power, he or she can also develop the mentality that whatever he or she does is right and that people are there to follow and support his or her wants, desires, and choices.

The god-like complex is developed when we receive praise, admiration, and worship from people and don't redirect it back to God. In essence, we are blocking God from his worship. God is displaying his power in us through the unique and amazing abilities he has given us, much like the power he gave to his apostles in the early centuries of Christianity. However, unlike those followers who deflected all god-like worship from people away from themselves with indignation (Acts 14:8-19), we have been absorbing that worship instead of redirecting it to God—even though he is the only one deserving of it and the only one able to handle it because he created us to worship him.

If a god-like complex is developing in individuals of status and power, then it is being partially created by those who exalt them to such heights. Often overlooked in how the powerful behave is how the less powerful admire and follow the views, ideas, and behaviors of those in power. The love affair of the less powerful toward the powerful often becomes the greatest single influence in an individual's life. It is the feelings we have of supporting, following, and uplifting those we admire so deeply that begin to shape and create a worship culture in all walks of human society.

Chapter 5: If Loving You Is Wrong...

At one point, *American Idol* was one of the biggest and most successful shows on television. The premise was to find unknown musical talent and let America begin to fall in love with these musical artists as they competed to become the next American Idol. Today we see an easy depiction of how inappropriate worship has been changed by society into an accepted practice of admiration and support: it's common today for fans of sports figures and entertainers to refer to those they've admired, looked up to, or tried to imitate as their idols.

Young people today grow up in a world where status and power are clearly exalted in our society, and they look to those exalted individuals with such admiration that they begin to shape their values and behaviors around such people. We have given permission to ourselves as humanity to engage in a forbidden love affair that draws us to exalt people to places in our hearts where only God should reside.

I can easily recall in my younger years how the sports, music, and film industries shaped the culture of the African American community. During my youth, I would say it was the music industry that was most influential in transforming culture. Music artists, especially fellow African American artists, were so admired and revered by those of us who desired to live and experience their lives. They seemed to have it all—money, fame, devoted followers— you name it, they had it. They were sex symbols to the young and old alike. We idolized them. We felt that by listening to their music and living out their words given to us in song, we were in some way experiencing being a part of their lives. Their music was the Bible for the young community. We did what they said in their music because we idolized who they were.

If You Say So...

The problem was that the more we embraced their words, the less we embraced God's words. We were told there was nothing wrong with having premarital sex, sex at a young age, multiple sex partners, secret sex partners, and extramarital sex partners. As a result, the family nucleus, which was already fragile in our community, was shattered.

Babies were having babies, young people were dying of AIDS, and older men were often found sleeping with and impregnating middle and high school girls whom they flattered with their god-like status in the community as drug dealers, athletes, and thugs. We were told that selling drugs, rebelling against law enforcement, and killing others would make you more respected and admired by others. We were being given permission to become the idols of our own communities. The more we saw this as right, the more we understood God and church as being wrong, outdated, and not cool. The last thing you wanted to be labeled as back then was a church boy or church girl.

It is amazing how God's warning to his people Israel was really a warning for all of humanity to not allow ourselves to exalt anything or anyone in our hearts because they would lead us away from him. As a young man, I didn't disobey God because I didn't want to follow him; I disobeyed God because I was already following someone else. As I said earlier about admiration, when we have deep admiration for someone, we behave in such a way that supports or protects their views and ideology.

If those I idolized told me that living a certain way was right, then I began to champion that view in my life, even if it meant that it was going against God. You see, I had a god already, so it was as if the roles were reversed and God himself was trying be an idol in my life and pull me away from that which I already was worshiping—what a scary thought! Whoever or whatever we worship becomes our god by default. So what is the difference between a god and an idol? If you believe what or who you are worshiping is right, then that thing or person becomes your god. However, if you believe who or what you are worshiping is wrong, then that's your idol. The problem is that the only time you see an idol as wrong is when you are not worshiping it.

I believe in the God of the Bible, but so did the people in the Bible who knew him before I did and much longer than I have, and yet they still turned away at times and served foreign gods. Why was this possible? This was possible because whoever or whatever has your heart, mind, and soul will have your allegiance. This is why God commanded his people to allow their hearts, minds, and souls to be captivated by him and him alone.

When the crowd saw what Paul had done, they shouted in the Lycaonian language, "The gods have come down to us in human form!"... But when the apostles Barnabas and Paul heard of this, they tore their clothes and rushed out into the crowd, shouting: "Friends, why are you doing this? We too are only human, like you..." Even with these words, they had difficulty keeping the crowd from sacrificing to them. ~Acts 14:11–15; 18

When we marvel at the amazingness of people, their status, acclaim, and accomplishments are supposed to make us more awed about God (the gift/ability giver) who created them and gave them such potential. Instead, we tend to marvel at the people (the gift recipients) and not God. Wrong worship is to worship and serve the created things as opposed to the creator of those things (Acts 1:25). The more impressed we are with people, the more we admire them and the more inclined we are to begin to worship them. We are always looking for something or someone to express our worship toward.

45

Only Human

In Acts 14, Paul did something amazing! So much so that he had the people raving about it. They were so impressed with what Paul did that they gave him and Barnabas the status of gods. How would you feel if someone idolized you as if you were a god? What if they worshiped you, valued your every word, supported every action, willingly conformed to every request—and felt honored and privileged in doing so? Would you be flattered by such treatment? Paul and Barnabas were not at all flattered; in fact, they were quite the opposite!

The Bible tells us that they were indignant—so indignant that they felt an immediate sense of grief and mourning, which they expressed by the custom of tearing their clothes. This practice was common among Jews during intense feelings of grief and sorrow, as with the death of a loved one or acknowledgement and brokenness of sin committed toward God. In other words, two key leaders of the early church were showered with praise and exaltation, and they responded as if someone had died!

46

Why such a response? Why not just say, "Hey, we are flattered by your compliments and support, but we are just doing what God would have us do"? These leaders had been through so many tragic situations, as recorded in the Bible and I'm sure many others that were not recorded, and yet we see that it was during a time when they received high praise, admiration, and exaltation that they mourned the most.

I believe the severity of their response gives us an idea of how seriously they took the situation. To them, of all the things they had experienced, this situation was turning out to be one of the most tragic if not the most tragic situations they had ever experienced. Their actions resulted in a region of people violating the first and second commandments! They were indignant because their actions were creating idolizers and not God worshipers. In their eyes and according to scripture, one could argue that there is not a more serious offense. To add insult to injury, this was happening as a result of how the group of people were responding to Paul's and Barnabas' status and display of power.

I, John, am the one who heard and saw these things. And when I had heard and seen them, I fell down to worship at the feet of the angel who had been showing them to me. But he said to me, "Don't do that! I am a fellow servant with you and with your fellow prophets and with all who keep the words of this scroll. Worship God!" ~Revelation 22:8–9

The danger here is that temptation toward wrong worship doesn't just happen to those whom some may consider gullible, like the people in Lystra. We see from the above passage that even the apostle John, who had been with Jesus and had seen his power and divinity, was so moved by his experience with the angel during his revelation that even he was compelled to worship him. We also read how adamant the angel was at redirecting the praise and worship to whom it was intended: God. This perfectly illustrates that no one is above worship gone wrong. As leaders of people or individuals of great status and influence, we must be careful to not allow ourselves to get caught up in the feelings of flattery that we establish within ourselves or allow ourselves to become objects of worship.

The challenge I face, as do many other leaders or people of influence in the world, is how to lead others without becoming intoxicated or attracted to their praise of us, their admiration of us, their willingness and desire to follow us. I believe the answer lies in not just remaining humble but remaining human. You see, praise and adoration from our fellow men doesn't just affect our humility; it affects our humanity. It begins to make us feel more like a god and less like a human. What keeps us humble is not remembering how bad or sinful we are, but knowing how powerful, wonderful, and holy God is and how powerless we are. It is our humanity that will keep us humble—our true convictions that we are only instruments through which power is being displayed. We are mere puppets, and the true awe and wonder lies with the puppet master. It is he who gives life to the puppet and enables it to do anything.

We must all guard our hearts and make sure we are directing our deepest feelings of admiration and praise to God and him alone. We must always be reminded as the angel reminded John that we are all servants, regardless of our status ranks or levels of power. Worship is a two-way street. When powerful individuals are using their power and influence on the unwilling, less powerful, that's called abusive use of power, or tyranny. When the less powerful are expressing an intense admiration and allegiance to the unwilling but powerful individual, this can be seen as an obsession or fanaticism. However, when both sides engage in or allow such behavior, it creates a type of magnetic pull of the powerful and powerless towards one another that eventually becomes worship.

We have to ask ourselves some honest questions. Are we creating or engaging in an atmosphere of wrong worship, either as the worshiper or the one being worshiped? Either way, we see by the actions of the early church leaders and from the angel of God that such behavior is of the most tragic kind. The next chapter will look deeper into what makes wrongly directed worship so wrong.

Chapter 7: Obsessions & Addictions

Worship is powerful. It reinforces the human relationship between the powerful and the less powerful. The stronger the worship relationship, the more difficult it is to break. The human worship relationship is strengthened by obsessions and addictions to power and status. Obsessions can develop from the privilege that the less powerful feel from engaging in social relationships with individuals of high power and status. Less powerful people love the feeling of being known or valued by someone much higher than themselves. The more attention the powerful show the less powerful, the more the less powerful will desire such attention. The danger is that eventually, the less powerful person becomes so dependent on being in a social relationship with the powerful that he or she behaves in whatever ways are needed to preserve or strengthen the exchange relationship.

Addiction to status and power is the silent killer of many church pastors and spiritual leaders. Being on the receiving end of constant approval, praise, and devotion from followers activates the same reward-seeking chemicals in the brain as do other pleasure-seeking activities. In other words, spiritual leaders are often living under the influence of status and power, which can not only distort their judgment but also escalate into an addiction. When you combine the obsessions of followers with the addictions of leaders, you have the formula for a worship relationship. The more these two powerful forces interact, the stronger the pull toward one another becomes. The stronger the pull, the more both the leader and follower engage in behaviors that reinforce the worship dynamic between them.

Celebrity Culture in Churches

We live in a celebrity culture where we have become fascinated by the fame and acclaim of the world's most visible figures. With the advancement of media and technology, the social hierarchies of status in the world have become a natural part of modern society. The more we see of a person on TV or the Internet or hear of them on the air waves or news, the more he or she becomes elevated in our consciousness. We reason that these people must be of importance because they have the attention of the world.

There are a couple of ways one achieves the status of a celebrity. How well known someone is to the masses can create a national or international popularity that results in their recognition as a celebrity. On an individual level, how high someone exalts an individual in his or her own mind and hearts can turn someone into a type of celebrity for him or her personally. Celebrity status can have less to do with how visible an individual is and more to do with how high he or she is placed in the minds and hearts of individual people. The number of people praising them doesn't matter when it comes to being viewed as a celebrity; what matters is how much they are praised by an individual.

The rock-star status has gone mainstream and is prevalent in all walks of society. From sports and entertainment to politics and business, those most visible and in positions of status and power are treated like celebrities in their own right. The sad reality is that the religious world has not been immune to this growing trend. Today, mega church leaders, preachers, Christian entertainers, and spiritual leaders of all kinds are experiencing the same rock-star elevation as their secular world contemporaries. They mingle with the social elite, are called upon to address significant spiritual matters, and are as visible in many regards as some of the world's most visible figures.

In the church world, this celebrity status has an added dose of elements that make it even more powerful: trust and vulnerability. Not only can church followers place leaders high in their hearts, they also trust at a higher level, whatever the behaviors are of the leader. Such followers are also more vulnerable and willingly influenced by the thoughts, actions, and behaviors of those they have come to deeply praise and admire. As mentioned earlier, the results of such a combination are often tragic.

Leaders who are so revered often have nothing stopping them from giving in to the temptation of using their influence and power to gratify their desires. To them and to those who are enamored by them, their behaviors are not wrong. It is of no surprise then why many of the moral failings reported in churches are said to happen within church leader and church member relationships. It should also come as no surprise that the leaders most often involved in such behavior are the senior pastors and worship leaders—the most visible and recognized positions in most congregations.

Similar to the Paul and Barnabas experience mentioned earlier, many of today's spiritual leaders are being praised by their followers at dangerous levels of admiration. However, unlike Paul and Barnabas, many of them are accepting the high praise as opposed to redirecting it back to God. Unknown to many of them, as a result of not refusing high praise, they are becoming addicted to the feeling of being exalted in the minds and hearts of their followers. In the next couple of chapters, I want to specifically address what I believe is the most common, and in my opinion, the most intense worship relationship we see in most churches today: the worship relationship between the male leader and the female follower.

Warning: Proceed with Caution

Most churchgoers would not see themselves as worshiping something or someone other than God. However, based on the core definition of worship, many are unaware that their behavior reveals that they have placed man and or things above God in their lives. Many would argue that they are merely obeying the scriptures and submitting to the authority of their leaders or striving to make their leaders work a job rather than a burden. I will admit that it can be very difficult to discern if a relationship is mere follower obedience or human worship. We usually recognize that what we thought was obedience was actually worship after following such individuals has led to regretted behavior or accepted behavior. So how can we tell if we have begun to worship something or someone other than God?

When we begin to justify our behavior not by the Holy Spirit or the word of God but solely by the ideas or behaviors of someone else, we are in dangerous territory. Remember this is what admiration can do to us—influence us to behave in a ways that supports and protects the ideas and actions of those we admire.

When leaders fail to recognize their humanity and don't submit to the Holy Spirit, God's word, and other spiritual leaders, they likely have exalted themselves in their own hearts or have been exalted in the hearts of others.

When this happens, leaders began to lose sight of God's dominion over their lives. They portray themselves more as representatives of God as opposed to servants and slaves of God. You see, when someone is exalted, he or she can't really fake humility. Very rarely will they seek guidance or accountability, but they will be big on holding others accountable. We need to be aware of the signs of falling into worship as followers and the signs of leaders becoming the objects of our worship.

Chapter 8: Worship Dangers—Male Leaders

The worship of powerful, influential men who have high status creates a dangerous dynamic for both those who worship them and those who are being worshiped. I want to specifically address a real growing crisis in the Christian world: the moral failings of influential men. Men of high status, power, and influence often engage in moral and ethical failings because of the development of the god-like complex. With God, there is no such thing as the impossible; the Bible tells us that everything is possible with God. The danger of the god-like complex is that human men also begin to believe that there are no limitations to what they can do, have, or be.

Research over the years has shown that the more power you have, the more inclined you are to use that power. In the same way that God is always right, sinful men who have been exalted to great heights can lose their sense of humanity and begin to see all they do or desire as being both permissible and possible. I hope you can see where I am going with this. Being worshiped by another person creates the worst possible combination—one that deserves nothing now believes that he is entitled to any and everything.

Exalting man in a worship relationship creates in them an almost automatic drive to pursue and act upon their desires. The danger is the reality that as people, and as men, we have sinful desires, which in Christ, we are called to fight against or flee from. However, when a man is given great status and power, he is influenced to pursue his desires because of the great probability he has of actually obtaining them with little or no perceived consequences. This is the danger of the god-like complex.

As mentioned earlier, individuals of high status and power often engage in moral and ethical failings because of the development of the god-like complex. In the same way that God has no moral or ethical boundaries because he is God, men who are being worshiped can lose their sense of moral and ethical boundaries. Those in their social circles often begin to support and cater to the behavior of the powerful out of intense admiration, love, or devotion for the person with power. Imagine living life with no perceived limits; this turns sinful desires into realistic, obtainable goals. I believe that spiritual men of influence are falling into sexual sins with women more often because they can than because they want to. It's amazing how much desires can change when possibilities are increased. It's one thing to say I don't desire something; it is a whole different animal to say I can easily have something if I chose to, but I am choosing not to have it.

Let's talk about sex. Sex is a real drive for men. Men were made to have sexual desires that are meant to be fulfilled by their wives. However, because of our sinful violation of the purity of sex, today we seek the pleasure of sex without the responsibility of sex. When we exalt spiritual men to god-like status, they become more likely to engage in sexual pursuits than someone who is not exalted. Again this is because their mentality tells them that they can have that which seems unattainable to most. When the possibilities are increased, the temptation is also increased. King David is the perfect example of how sexual sins can happen with men of power and status—not so much because they want to, but more because they are able to.

One evening David got up from his bed and walked around on the roof of the palace. From the roof he saw a woman bathing. The woman was very beautiful, and David sent someone to find out about her. The man said, "She is Bathsheba, the daughter of Eliam and the wife of Uriah the Hittite." Then David sent messengers to get her. She came to him, and he slept with her...Then she went back home.
~2 Samuel 11:2–4

King David was without question a man of status and power. As we read, the king had no initial intentions of sleeping with the woman next door. However, when he encountered the unplanned sight of an attractive women bathing, both his sinful nature and god-like complex kicked in. First, we can say he was sexually enticed by what his eyes saw. At this point, the sinful flesh was rearing its ugly head. Unlike Joseph, son of Jacob, who fled his sexual temptation, King David pursued his.

As mentioned earlier, when we exalt people, we begin to support, protect, and enable their ideas and behaviors. Here we see that because of his status as king, people seemed to do whatever he asked them to do with any hesitation. Being on the outside of the situation as readers, it can be easy for us to say how wrong it was for them to comply and how they did not stand up for righteousness. I would argue that many of us, if placed in the presence of the most powerful man in a kingdom (or even a democracy for that matter), unfortunately would have done the same. He was the king.

If there was not admiration or love of the king, there was surely devotion to him as the man exalted on the throne. The problem with this tragic situation was that in the moment, the only person capable of stopping this act from taking place was the same person who was in full pursuit of making it happen: King David himself. No one seems to tell the king no or even question why he is inquiring about the women next door. Even Bathsheba herself was placed in such a tough situation as to be pursued sexually by the man who was above her own husband. King David didn't pursue Bathsheba because he wanted to; he pursued her because he could—because there was nothing and no one to stop him from doing so. He didn't even know who she was initially, but as we see, who she was became irrelevant (a good friend's wife) to what he had the power to do. It was the fact that he knew he could sleep with her that turned the king's temptation into a pursued goal.

For men of power, temptations are much different than temptations for people with less power. The exalted men of status and power knowingly have a realistic opportunity to get what they desire, and so their temptations can quickly turn into a full pursuit because they typically have all green lights along the way. Men of less power can have the same temptations, but because of their realistic limitations, they will never pursue those temptations. I tell people it's easy to say you will never cheat on your wife with a supermodel—until you have supermodels wanting you to cheat on your wife with them. What we now realize is that for individuals in exalted positions of status and influence, it takes a lot less than we think it would for them to engage in behaviors we think they could never do.

All it takes is a spark to set the pursuit of the exalted on a blazing course. It could be words of flattery, support, or admiration that get the ball rolling. It could be expressed vulnerability by a woman that starts things down the wrong path. Or it could be the constant green lights that the spiritual man perceives of his actions that keep him advancing forward to a place of no return. What we know is that men without such status and influence do not have the same opportunities given to them compared to those men who are exalted by status and influence.

We must be careful to help men of status by not treating them like gods, which will in turn help them not become captive to their abilities to pursue their desires, especially when those desires are sinful in nature. Please understand that I am not condoning or justifying any behavior that individuals have committed or will commit in the future. I am trying to express how much of a role that human worship often plays in the fall of exalted men from great heights.

Chapter 9: Worship Dangers—Female Followers

Research studies have shown that women are known to be attracted to the status of a man. In my doctoral research about status and power's influence on sexual behavior of male college football players, I was somewhat surprised by how high-status males described most women they encountered. They believed their status made them more attractive to women than a normal, non-sport playing college male. In fact, they said women were so attracted to their status as football players that oftentimes it was the women who were pursuing them and not the other way around. Women are attracted to high status men outside the church, and they are attracted to the status of men inside the church. Combined with the influence on men in the previous chapter, I firmly believe these are the ingredients for many of the adulterous/immoral sexual sins that happen among male church leaders and female followers.

But realize this, that in the last days difficult times will come. For men will be lovers of self...lovers of pleasure rather than lovers of God, holding to a form of godliness, although they have denied its power; Avoid such men as these. For among them are those who enter

into households and captivate weak women weighed down with sins,
led on by various impulses… ~2 Timothy 3:1–6

Paul talks about men who use their spiritual influence to seduce women into sin. He mentions some things here that I think are important to point out. First, it seems implied that these men used their portrayal of spirituality as a means to get in the door. I have observed in my time as a Christian that Christian women tend to be more vulnerable and less guarded around Christian men. The more "spiritual" or the higher status they are as men, the more vulnerable and less guarded many women seem to be. This becomes the open door for the relationship to go south fast. The next thing he points out is that these men enter their homes. In other words, the closer the proximity, the greater the influence.

Studies have shown that a female can develop an emotional attachment to a male just from being in close proximity to him. Long hugs have also been said to create attachment bonds in women. The thing with these types of emotional attachments is they make women extremely trusting of the man they are becoming attached to. This creates the vulnerable presence a woman can have, which often become an enticing, attractive vibe to men who interpret the vulnerability as a wanting to be pursued.

For women, it is important to be aware of the emotional and behavioral influence the status and power of male leaders can have over them if they allow it. Female attachment is much different than male attraction. With men, most attraction is physical. Some men are also drawn to women who are submissive because it reinforces their male dominance, while others are drawn to that which seems forbidden or unobtainable because they are drawn to the excitement of the challenge. Women, on the other hand, are more built for emotional bonding than men. Women can develop strong emotional bonds from everything from long hugs, holding hands, conversations, and merely being in close presence with someone.

Oftentimes it is the bonds that are built that create strong emotional connections among women followers with men leaders. For example, a woman speaks to a pastor about a spiritual situation in which he provides insight and help. The female church member is grateful for the help, praising the leader for his wisdom and care to take time out to help. The woman returns periodically when needed to get spiritual guidance from the male spiritual leader. However, the more they meet and discuss things at a personal level, the more the attachment bond is being developed. Eventually both parties are now on autopilot in their being drawn to interact with one another. The mutually rewarding feelings experienced by both individuals blind them to what objective individuals would consider behavior of growing concern. The interaction eventually becomes more frequent and intimate as the *vulnerable and emotionally attached* behavior of the woman gives a green light to the *nothing wrong with what I am doing* behavior of the male leader. As many would term it, one thing leads to another, and the interaction culminates in the highest level of social intimacy: sex.

Understand that I am more than aware that on either side, there are those who are just wolves in sheep's clothing who knowingly attempt to gratify their desires. However, many of them didn't start out that way; they were enslaved by the allure of status and power, which became worship. Many of the situations I have heard about often describe the woman as selfish and trying to destroy the happy home of the pastor. However, what many do not understand is that status and power can spark emotional feelings of admiration quickly and at intense levels, often sweeping a woman into an entanglement she never intended to happen in the first place.

Women must guard their hearts at all costs in order to not be enticed to exalt men leaders in their hearts to such a place that it tempts them to bow down in their hearts in worship of them. Female worship of male leaders doesn't start with them pursuing the leader sexually; it usually starts with them becoming captivated by the leader and expressing it through praise and increased vulnerability. It is praise and devotion from the opposite sex that becomes an attractive thing to the powerful male, often leading him to pursue more praise and become vulnerable to their own fleshly desires. The end result of moral failures between the woman and man are often the byproduct of worship gone wrong. Restoring worship to the way it is supposed to be will implement corrective measures on the part of both the powerful and those influenced by their power.

Chapter 10: Worship & Worship Leaders

The Power of Music

Music has power. God created music and gave it a fundamental role in worship in the Old Testament. I am not professing to be a music expert; however, from reading 1 Chronicles, we see that musicians and singers were a large part of the worship experience. The Bible tells us the musicians *ministered* with music. This tells us that they served God and served the people or met the needs of the people through music. I can imagine the presence and the experience of hearing a grand orchestra and choir. The atmosphere had to be powerful. This scene is but a snippet of what we will experience and the sounds we will hear in the presence of God. Music has the power to teach our hearts at the emotional level and enhance our experience in the moment—for better or for worse.

When I was a kid playing Pop Warner football for the Florida City Razorbacks, we traveled from Homestead, Florida, to Orlando to play a football classic game against a team from Chicago. Needless to say, we won big! However, my point was that I can remember being in the Disney area for the first time and staying in a hotel for almost a week. We were away from the drugs, the fights, the condemned and abandoned houses—we were living it up with the mouse! I just remember having so much fun that I didn't want it to be over. When the time came for us to depart, we were loading the bus to get on the road. I remember as I was making my way to my seat, the chorus of a song came on over the radio that brought me to tears. The song was *Time of My Life* by Bill Medley and Jennifer Warnes. The words moved my heart as I heard:

> *I've had the time of my life*
> *No I never felt this way before*
> *Yes I swear it's the truth*
> *And I owe it all to you*

The song was speaking to me about how I felt about my time in Orlando. I had the time of my life and never wanted to leave. I felt I owed it all to being in Orlando. I didn't want to go back home and return to the hard life we were living as youth. I cried quietly in my seat. I was so moved by the song and how it spoke to me as a 6th grade kid that I made a commitment right then that one day, I was going to come back to this place. Well sure enough when I graduated high school, my wife and I moved to Orlando for college (Go Knights!), and we never left. Think about it; the music had such a profound impact on how I felt that a few seconds of hearing it changed the course of my life. All I could remember was that Orlando was the place where I had the time of my life. As a result, it became the place I wanted to spend the rest of my life; so far, so good.

That was the pretty side of how music influenced my life. Unfortunately there are many more examples of how music influenced me in ways I am not proud of and wish I could take back. I have felt hate for people, mistreated and devalued women, and attempted to live a street life—all actions that were greatly influenced by the music I listened to religiously as a youth. I had no doubt that music was meant to influence our feelings, thoughts, attitudes, and behaviors. We can hear a certain song and immediately be taken back to significant moment (good or bad) in our lives where we heard the song being played. This is no different when it comes to spiritual music or music in the church. However, in the same way I was moved by the music to follow its message and its messenger, Christian artists and music leaders in churches today have a similar power within them.

Loyal Followers

Social media has given us a glimpse into how serious we are as a society about following people of high status. At the time of this writing, according to Twitaholic.com and Twittercounter.com, the person with the largest Twitter following is the musical artist Justin Bieber, with over 42.7 million followers. That is roughly 13 percent of the U.S. population! To put this in more perspective, that is over 8 million more social followers than the man who actually leads the U.S. population: President Barack Obama. In fact, 4 of the top 5 and 7 of the top 10 Twitter followings belong to music artists. Only the President, YouTube, and Instagram happen to be 3 of the top 10 social followings that are not music artists. This is the power of music; music can create a following.

Music creates followers because music touches lives. Remember, I am writing this from my home office in Orlando partly because of music I heard for a few seconds over 20 years ago. Musicians are some of the top worshiped individuals in the world. With some of the world's top musicians, the phrases "I idolized you" or "You were my idol" are used as positive expressions of the deep admiration people have for them. This powerful concept of musicians exalted in the hearts of people is no different in the church.

A key component to worship developing with musicians is visibility. With the influence of music on our hearts combined with an incredible amount of exposure and visibility, musical artists can become some of the most admired and followed individuals in the world. At a more local and personal level, this takes place with our musicians in churches as a result of their frequent and significant visibility among churchgoers. Singers, worship leaders, and musicians touch the hearts of churchgoers more intimately and over a longer period of time than most church pastors. It is thus no surprise that musical worship leaders can be just as if not more exalted in the hearts of Christ followers than any other church leader. As a result, worship leaders have become a constant object of worship in many churches today.

As people often follow their most admired music artist—be it through social media or traveling to tours in person—church people often follow church musicians. Today, music can be a main reason people come to particular church and a main reason they leave a particular church. One of the reasons in my early years that I didn't care much about church was because I often saw how much power the music person had in the church. Musicians seemed like hot commodities, and churches were fighting for their services. Church leaders even back then knew that people came and followed a good musician. In fact, where I grew up, most of the animosity between churches had to do with one church trying to take away a worship leader from another church! What I saw as a result was music people who had influential status and power in churches—and with status and power came unhealthy freedoms and celebrity-like treatment.

Free & Often Feared

Many worship leaders are often held unaccountable because church leaders they are blinded to the outside signs that show there is an inside issue. Sin does not make a worship leader sound worse; it doesn't affect their God-given ability to hold a note. This is why accountability is so vital when it comes to worship leaders. The more they touch us deeply through music, the less inclined we are to remember that they are only human, like the rest of us. Similar to secular artists with live show performances, worship leaders feel the pressure and responsibility to show up and "perform," even when their hearts may not be in a healthy place. On the other hand, some musical worship leaders use the church stage as a way to receive immediate praise and adoration from followers. This helps them numb the pain and escape or avoid the real issues weighing on their hearts that have gone unconfessed and unaddressed. Sunday singing for some worship leaders sadly has become their drug of choice.

Many leaders have become paralyzed in their ability to give spiritual help to worship leaders. They often struggle with addressing the sins or shortcomings of those in charge of their music worship due to the significant following and support they have among church members. Often this is because leaders have turned blind eyes to the worship leaders because of the positive influence they are having on the church experience. Also, it is because leaders fear the fallout that losing a great music leader can have on their church. When a church leader feels the need to tread lightly with addressing the lives of their music leaders because of how it will affect the church, they fail to realize that they have allowed themselves and the church to worship the worship leader.

Not only do we kill churches by catering to talented musicians because they can put and keep people in the seats, but we often kill the spirituality of the musicians themselves. In churches we are often setting our musical leaders up for moral and spiritual failures because we are exalting them in our hearts and worshiping them with our behavior. We send them mixed messages with our behavior. While their lives may be in a mess, we have come to treat musical worship leaders with more *"grace"* than we do others whose lives are not as messed up. The only real difference is that they are not worship leaders. This treatment tells worship leaders that they are more valuable than others and influences them to not seeing their sins and shortcomings as honestly as they should. However, we can't expect them to see their own faults soberly when those of us who lead them and listen to them aren't spiritually consistent in how we help them to be righteous.

The Bible tells us that music and music leaders were important to the worship experience; however, they were never the focal point of the experience. Music leaders, along with every other leader when it came to God, were ministers—nothing more, nothing less. They were there to minister, which means to serve in whatever capacity God placed them in to do so. Today we have to find a way to return the roles of worship leaders and other church leaders back to being servants that enhance our worship and not celebrities that are focus of our worship.

Chapter 11: The ALMIGHTY Dollar

Those who want to get rich fall into temptation and a trap and into many foolish and harmful desires that plunge people into ruin and destruction. For the love of money is a root of all kinds of evil. Some people, eager for money, have wandered from the faith and pierced themselves with many griefs. ~1Timothy 6:9–10

This revelation given to me about worship and money has been a bit more challenging to put down on paper than the other chapters. It's a challenge because there is a lot of following of breadcrumbs trails that's necessary in order to arrive at our destination. Therefore it is important that you stay with me on this one. It may be a good idea to process this chapter slowly over a few days if needed so the words and examples can begin to take root and make more sense with time, study, and prayer.

A Package Deal

Worship and service are a package deal. As I have mentioned throughout this book, who or what we worship influences who we are and what we do. Worship influences behavior. There is no worship if there is no servant or service. At one end of the worship relationship is God or that which has been placed as a god (idolatry) in our lives; this is the master. At the other end of the worship relationship, we have the servant who serves its master in a worship relationship. Thus when Jesus rebuked Satan when he was being tempted, he tells him that we are to worship God and serve him only (Matthew 4:10). So based upon this understanding, it is very possible to determine who or what we worship by discovering who or what we serve in an exalted way.

In Matthew 6, Jesus tells us that money has the potential of becoming a master—a god in our lives. Money has this potential for several reasons. One reason is that money is associated with status; the more money you have, the higher your social status typically is. Second, money is a form of access. By access I mean it opens doors or removes obstacles in ways that other materials things cannot. Lastly, money is a form of power. The combination of being highly recognized, having a great degree of access, and having great opportunities creates social power. In one sense, social power in the ability to influence people and situations by having more control over resources than others.

All of these characteristics reflect the characteristics of God: high in status, access, and power. Money can become a god because money has the ability to mimic God in our society. It can do pretty much all the things that God can do from a materialistic standpoint. Thus because of its capabilities, money itself is easily and often exalted to god-like status. We exalt money because it has the ability to exalt us.

Jesus also makes the connection between worship and service when it comes to a master, be it God or money. He says whomever we have as master is the person we will love, be devoted to, and serve. Love, devotion, and service to a master is what we call worship. Take away any of those characteristics, and it is no longer a worship relationship. In other words, whoever is our master is who we will worship. The word *serve* in Matthew 4:10 and 6:24 is referring to our behaviors and actions being dictated by the exalted master in our lives. This is different than serving one another or being a servant to those in need. Serving in the way just described is not dictated by the one being served. However, serving someone exalted above us is totally dictated by the one being served.

This is why Jesus says that we are to serve God only. He tells us that God is the only one we are to serve in such a way that he dictates who we are and what we do; this is the true definition of worship service. Jesus is saying that money, when placed in an exalted place in our hearts, can begin to dictate who we are and what we do. If money can become a god in our hearts, then money can be worshiped.

How Can You Tell?

When your decisions become more financially dictated than faith or God based, you are serving money, not God. This is so important to understand because I truly believe many of us as church leaders and churchgoers are in a worship relationship with money, and we either don't realize it or don't care. Some will argue that making financial decisions is not wrong, but wise—in fact, that makes us good stewards. My response is that financial decisions are right in the same way that any other decision can be right. The difference, however, is that money is directly associated with access, status, and power; when money is the final or major determining factor of what we do or don't do, who we listen to or don't listen to, and who we follow or don't follow, then make no mistake about it— we are serving and thus worshiping money.

I have observed today how deeply entrenched the church has become in money worship. It seems that now more than ever, the major dictating factor in churches is money. Rarely does anyone want to talk about the elephant in the living room; that's probably because we don't want to accept the reality that we were the ones who brought it in the house in the first place! Money today dictates if the gospel is shared or if churches are planted. Last I checked, Jesus did not say, "Go make disciples of all nations—that is, if it's in the budget."

Money has also dictated the status a church has in society. Many churches today display their financial prowess similar to that of Fortune 500 companies. We reason that people are drawn to what they are impressed by, and the more money we have, the more impressive we can be for God—that's what we tell ourselves, even though it's really how impressive we can be in the eyes of man. This is the corporate worldview that has infiltrated the church. In the corporate world, there is no question who runs the show: it's the almighty dollar. The corporate world is about revenue; that is where cash is king, and you are legally obligated to make decisions dictated by the responsibility one has to making money.

The church has seen the influence money has had in the secular world and has been enticed to seek the same influence in the church. We make it okay by telling ourselves that it is God who is giving us the money, so it must be in his will. Scripture tells us that when God is no longer the final say, then God has stopped being God in our lives. God gives us money, but God does not need to give us money for him to dictate our service to him. In fact, money is not the issue; the issue is who is getting the glory, credit, and praise? When we make decisions dictated by money, we are saying that the money is responsible for the success, opportunity, or outcome and thus deserves the credit, glory, and praise.

I remember when my wife and I were called by God to start Unus Solutions, Inc., which is the parent organization of True River Ministries. God has made it clear that we were not to go into full-time work jobs but were to supplement our income with part-time work to leave time for us to build the ministry he called us to. We left paid ministry positions and started this ministry with no job to transition into. The question we often got from friends and fellow church members was "How will you pay the bills and take care of your family?" My answer—that if God called us to this ministry, he was going to provide—sounded like crazy talk, even irresponsible talk coming from a husband with two kids (one a newborn) and a wife who was still recovering from a life-threatening pregnancy. Most seemed to imply, without actually saying it directly, that our decisions needed to be sounder, that is, more financially based. However, God was asking us in our hearts who we were going to serve. Who were we going to allow to dictate the choices we make in our lives; would it be God, or would it be money?

We said God, but we later began to realize that there was some money worship even in our own lives that we had not been aware of. On our journey, God was showing himself faithful to us constantly, yet for some reason, we were still uneasy each month when money ran low, when an illness happened in the family, or when an unexpected expense popped up. We couldn't understand why we were not more joyful and excited about how God was constantly providing for us, until one day he revealed to us the reason.

We were talking about this issue one day, as we seemed to do from time to time, when the question was posed in my heart: "Would you be more comfortable with God taking care of you and not giving you money or with God giving you the money and you taking care of yourself?" Our honest answer was that we were more comfortable and much preferred for God to give us the money as opposed to him providing for our needs without giving us money. What this said to us what that we were more dependent on and felt more need for money than God. This broke us spiritually as we realized that in reality, money was our security, provider, and protector; money was our God.

God didn't give us money because he was trying to heal us and bring us to repentance for serving money over him. We acknowledged that even as spiritual leaders, we had reasoned for a while why we could or could not do things based upon money or finances. We had seen other people be paralyzed when it came to faith because their faith was in the facts, and the facts were that the more money you had, the more you could do, and the less money you had, the less you were able to do. We had often ministered to and challenged believers on their lack of faith, only to realize that our faith and worship of God was not as strong as we originally thought.

God took us over the next two years and removed the dependency on money from our hearts. This allowed us to truly thank him for all of his wondrous and miraculous provisions he made for us time and time again, even to this very day. Many don't follow God in devoted obedience today because God does not have the final say in their lives; money does. When money has the final say in our lives, we are pulled into a constant pursuit of more of it, because the more money we have, the more secure we feel, and the more we tell ourselves we can listen to God now because we have the ability (money) to do so.

Chapter 12: Worship Is Big Business

Unfortunately, worship has and will continue to be a married to business agendas and motives. We read in Acts 19 a chilling yet all too familiar discourse from a silversmith named Demetrius. Demetrius gathers what could be considered something of a trade union to address a serious issue facing their economy and the stability of jobs in their region: a guy by the name of Paul. Paul's preaching of the gospel in the province of Asia was turning people toward worshiping God and, as a result, away from worshiping the temple goddess Artemis. As a public speaking instructor, I have to admit that this guy Demetrius was excellent at delivering a persuasive speech. One of the key elements to a persuasive speech is pathos—a Greek term referring to an emotional appeal to one's audience. Engaging someone emotionally means connecting with them at a heart level, appealing to that which they can personalize internally.

Demetrius does this brilliantly in his argument against Paul's turning people away from this goddess to the Lord. The silversmith pulls all of these individuals together who make their living from the people's worship of

Artemis. They provide the shrines for worship and other related items to help support and enhance the worship experience of the people. Demetrius gathers this group together and begins with this emotionally engaging statement in Acts 19:25:

"You know, my friends, that we receive a good income from this business."

Business is about supply and demand. Someone makes an income by supplying what the people are demanding with their purchase power. Although Demetrius' conversation would eventually address how Paul's teaching would turn people away from the goddess they valued, it started at the heart of it all; for them, worship was a business. Worship was their livelihood; it was how they put food on the table and roofs over their heads. This was not about whether or not Paul's teachings were accurate; this was solely about the ripple effect of his teachings and influence on their established economy.

This sadly is the same issue that prevents many from turning away from wrong worship in their lives. People have built livelihoods and businesses from wrong worship and refuse to lose or let go of what they have built. Let's face it; we know the disastrous impact of things such as drugs, pornography, obesity, sex, cigarettes, materialism, and much more on our society; yet the real reason they continue is because they are stabilizing components of our economy. Every day we see people's lives being destroyed by one or a combination of these societal norms; yet businesses continue to pump insane amounts of money into marketing these lifestyles to us in order to keep us worshiping them. They understand that the higher these things are exalted in our lives, the more we will spend money on them to support or enhance our experiences with them.

I recently mentioned to my wife how saddened and frustrated I was with our economic business model. We will tell anyone that our product or service works because we want their business, when oftentimes that not the case at all. People sell stuff more to make money for themselves than to add value to the consumer. We have moved away from societal cultivation into a culture of self-preservation.

I grew up around the drug selling of the 90s that was common in black communities. It was a clear example of how worship was a business. Seeing drug addicts out on the streets was a regular routine for me as a youth; in fact, not having a drug addict in your family was a foreign concept to all who grew up in low-income black communities. Just to paint the picture of how accepted drug worship was back then, for a long time when I was in middle school, the number one song played on the radio station was a song where little kids chanted the chorus that your mom was a crack cocaine addict.

Crack cocaine destroyed the black community in the late 80s and 90s. However, the business of being a crack seller was booming. People made a good income from supporting the worship of, and addiction to drugs in their own community. The money was so good and drug dealers took on such a high status in our communities that not only were addicts worshiping drugs, but the communities were worshiping drug dealers. When people would come in talking about saying no to drugs, they were threatening the economy that had become entrenched in many of our communities.

My example is no different than what is taking place in our society as a whole. We are being marketed to worship just about anything these days, especially if our worship can create income opportunities for someone else. What makes it even scarier is that it is justified by saying we are merely giving the people what they want. This makes sense as long as what they want supports what you are providing. Getting people back to worshiping God will be a fight, because to worship God means to stop worshiping something or someone else. When we stop worshiping someone else, we stop behaviors that many people have come to make a living from.

Let the Church Say Amen

Let's not kid ourselves and pretend that the business of worship has not affected the church as well. I believe this is one of the most detrimental issues facing churches today. In the pursuit of worshiping God, many have been redirected to worshiping "the church." The church leader, the church building, the church worship pastor—these are some of the good income areas that people are making a living off of in the body of Christ today. We often say, "What sets our church apart from the church down the street? How can we be different? What can we do to make people choose coming to our place instead of going somewhere else?" And just like Demetrius, we convince ourselves that it is a God thing when really, it's a money thing. We want more people in our seats because more people means more offerings, and more offerings means more things we can do to market more people coming.

When people are bringing a materialistic outlook on life into the church, we as leaders are not supposed to cater to or support it; we are supposed to turn them from false worshiping to worshiping God. Instead we see today that we have turned church life into big business, where many are competing for their share of the market. Why? Because they've made a livelihood out of doing church, and if they don't have people, they don't have a church. That is why it's no coincidence that most upstart churches' growth model is to bring people from existing churches by saying how they are different and just what they were looking for. I've heard things like, "This is not your grandmother's church" or "This is for people who are tired of church" or "We are a church for the next generation." What we fail to realize is that message we are sending people is to come and *worship us,* not come and worship *with* us.

When we do this, we as churches are no different than the market share wars played out on our TV screens between iPhone and Samsung, or Wal-Mart and Target, or McDonald and Burger King, and so many others. We too, like the secular companies, have evolved from societal cultivation in Christ to self-preservation in *our own* churches. The drug war of the 80s and 90s are no different than the business wars and church wars of today; the love of money has been and will continue to be the root of these evils.

The Leader Killer

Judas Iscariot was a leader. In fact, he was one of the highest founding leaders in church history—an apostle of Jesus. The Bible tells us that after spending all night in prayer with God, Jesus came and selected the twelve who would be designated Apostles. I can imagine Jesus in dialogue with his father about every single follower, going through them one by one, talking about their strengths and weaknesses and ultimately the plan that God would have for their lives. Judas was no less selected than Simon Peter, or any other apostle for that matter. If we are to truly understand the pitfalls that wrong worship can create, we must stop writing off Judas in our hearts as this corrupted man from the beginning. We must also take sober notice about many of our fallen spiritual leaders today; just like Judas, where they ended up was not where they started.

Jesus chose Judas. However, Judas would eventually choose money, power, and greed. We read in John 12 and 13 that Judas was in charge of the money for the ministry. I am not sure how they chose who would take on such an important role in a ministry; what we do see, however, is that such an important role was given to Judas. Was it because of the integrity he'd shown prior to being given such a role? Could it have been because of his gifted mind when it came to handling money? One thing is for sure; you don't have someone handle the money who can't handle the money! Judas was the man for the job. He was the leader chosen to have control and influence over the money of the ministry of Jesus.

Somewhere along the way, things went wrong. We read in John 12 that at some point, Judas began to help himself to the ministry's money. You would think if anyone were going to cheat someone, they would not try to cheat the man that has shown to be able to know and read a man's heart! Why would Judas even think to skim money from the ministry of God, especially when Jesus is the leader he was following? I believe the answer to this question is the same answer to why leaders today become corrupted and begin to make unrighteous decisions as if God was not there with them: they become gods themselves in their own hearts.

Like Judas the chosen leader, many church and spiritual leaders were chosen by God, only to fall because they went the wrong way in their worship. Money can corrupt any leader just as it did with Judas. It can make leaders believe they have the power, the capacity, and the right to make decisions the way they choose, even if they are contrary to God's commands. Don't get me wrong; I'm not saying that all spiritual leaders are stealing from the church. I am saying what causes leaders to make decisions that blatantly go against God is worship gone wrong. Judas' worship went wrong because of the influence money had on him. It became about the money, even to the point that he openly objected to what Jesus himself considered good use of a potential financial resource.

It is interesting how I have seen people be expelled from churches primarily for sexual sins, drug/substance use, or for actions found to be against the law. However, I don't think I've ever seen anyone in the church expelled— or even disciplined for that matter—for being greedy. Paul says the following in a passage often used for church discipline:

But now I am writing to you that you must not associate with anyone who claims to be a brother or sister but is sexually immoral or greedy, an idolater or slanderer, a drunkard or swindler. Do not even eat with such people. ~1 Corinthians 5:11

Paul goes a step further than just placing greed on the same level as inappropriate worship (idolatry); he actually refers to greed as idolatry itself:

Put to death, therefore, whatever belongs to your earthly nature: sexual immorality, impurity, lust, evil desires and greed, which is idolatry. Because of these, the wrath of God is coming. ~Colossians 3:5–6

The problem with greed is twofold. The first problem is that it is an inward heart condition that is not easily seen like other sins are, such as sexual immorality/adultery and drunkenness. The second problem is what makes the first problem worse: we have replaced the negative term of greed with many other positive terms, such as being prosperous, being goal driven, pursuing the American dream, and wanting a better life for our children. This allows greed to often go unchecked and undetected in the hearts and lives of churchgoers. Greed can take on many forms, from materialism of leaders and followers to spiritual favoritism and preferential treatment being shown to the wealthy within a congregation. When we have greed in our hearts when it comes to money, money and whoever has the money become our objects of worship, and this is idolatry.

I am not sure how to end this chapter because it seems the more I write, the more I want to write. Money, as Jesus has pointed out, can destroy people because it can begin to dictate who they are and how they live their lives. Those drug dealers in my community growing up didn't see that they were killing people; they saw that they were providing for their families and supporting the youth of the community in their own way. However, as with Judas, it was blood money—money that was giving them power and status at the expense of the lives and well-being of others. Let's do everything we can to prevent the dollar from becoming mightier than God in our lives, in our churches, and in our communities.

Chapter 13: The Worship War

"Now fear the LORD and serve him with all faithfulness. Throw away the gods your ancestors worshiped...But if serving the LORD seems undesirable to you, then choose for yourselves this day whom you will serve...But as for me and my household, we will serve the LORD." ~Joshua 24:14–15

The contents of this chapter were revealed to me in a dream during a nap (yes, I take naps!) one summer afternoon in Florida. As I lay in bed, I heard constant window-shaking thunder rolls vibrate my bedroom window. If you are familiar with Florida summer weather, you know that severe thunderstorms and even tornados can show up unexpectedly. My first thought was to go grab the kids from upstairs, check the weather channel, and get to a safe location; my wife and I are Hurricane Andrew survivors who lived through the eye of the storm in Homestead, Florida, so seeking shelter in storms had become second nature for us. However, this time, my spirit began to pray and praise God for his power that was on display. As I continued to lie there and pray in my spirit, the verses of a familiar song entered my heart:

"...I hear the rolling thunder, thy power throughout the universe displayed;

Then sings my soul, my savior God to Thee, How great thou art! How great thou art!"

That's when it hit me; I was experiencing the power of God that summer afternoon, and it moved me in my heart to praise and acknowledge God for his greatness. This is the war that is being waged today: the war on worship. The enemy knows that we were wired to worship power greater than ourselves. The more we see God's power, the more we are in awe of him, and the more we are inclined to worship him. When I heard the thunder that afternoon, my first instinct was to get up and make sure we were safe from the weather. What God was showing me was that my first inclination was to run from his power rather than be in awe of it.

The reason this is so important is that often, we fail to acknowledge the power of God that is on full display in the universe and in our lives. My first thought about the thunder was to refer to it as the weather and not the power of God. However, as I prayed and praised God during these incredible rumbles of thunder, I began to sense in my heart calmness mixed with vulnerability; I felt human. It was in my humanity that I felt drawn to God, amazed at his power and captivated by his presence. When we are exposed to the power of God, we are able to acknowledge that he and he alone is worthy of our worship. However, when we fail to recognize or acknowledge the power of God that's on display, we can in turn be pulled away by the power we see present in other people or other things. Thus the war on worship boils down to the enemy attempting to prevent us from worshiping God by distracting us from seeing God's power so we will follow and worship the lesser powers of this world.

You Decide

"...How long will you waver between two opinions? If the LORD is God, follow him; but if Baal is God, follow him." ~1 Kings 18:21

Elijah's showdown on Mount Carmel in 1 Kings 18 was a perfect example of a war on worship that was waged by the enemy through the sinfulness of mankind. God's prophet Elijah was one prophet against 850 prophets of Baal. The people were serving gods other than the Lord, and Elijah was tasked with turning that around. How could one prophet convince a nation to follow the god he was serving instead of the gods being served by the nearly 1,000 prophets before them at the time? The one way he could win was if this was a one-on-one fight—his god verses their god. You see, the enemy would like to keep the fight between people and opinions rather than bringing God's power into the mix.

What happened was that the people of Israel saw for themselves that the gods of the 850 prophets actually had no power. Their power came from the prophets telling the people that their gods had power. However, Elijah showed that the Lord God was really God, and the people fell down prostrate before him; they worshiped. It took God's power being seen in order for the false gods to be shown for who they really were—fakes gods, idols. I am convinced that this is also how the war on worship in our hearts is decided; whoever shows us real power wins.

Satan is distracting us from seeing the power of God by surrounding us with many voices telling us that power is found elsewhere. Since the only power we see is the manufactured power of man, we think that this is real power, and we follow it. Lately I have been more in the heart of Elijah, asking the Lord to show his power in the lives of believers and non-believers alike. Words without power are merely words, even if the words we are talking about come from the Bible. This is why Peter tells us that Jesus was accredited by God to us through miracles, wonders, and signs (Acts 2:22).

The power Jesus displayed by what he did gave credibility and validity to the things he said. In fact, if you read through the conversions in the book of Acts, you will find that God did something powerful through his disciples, and then they shared the message of the gospel, and people believed them and were baptized into Christ Jesus. This is where we have to go if we are to win the war on worship in the hearts of man. Elijah himself was outnumbered when it came to voices of reason; if the people were to choose between what he was saying and what the 850 prophets were saying, it was a no-brainer that they would go with the majority voice.

In the same way, we should not be surprised when our human efforts to convince people to follow God fall horribly short because the world is more convincing. Or when we feel the pressure in churches to keep up with the outside world in order to keep our people interested and more impressed with the church. The problem is that we're fighting human power with human power. In this type of fight, as with Elijah, we are usually outnumbered. What we have to do is take a page out of the lone prophet's fight strategy; let it be a one-on-one fight with God and whoever else wants to test him.

I have seen lately—more than in my earlier years in the faith—how prayer for God's power to intervene has won the battle time and time again. We have to stop trying to win the worship war with words, gimmicks, and programs and get on our knees and ask God to allow his power to be on full display so that people will have no question as to who they need to follow and worship.

Final Chapter: Restoring Worship

The act of spiritual worship is not a spiritual sacrifice. A sacrifice was a part of the worship relationship, but it was not the relationship. Today we have confused the worship act of offering a sacrifice with the modern idea that a sacrifice is something that's hard to do but that we're still obligated to do. To restore worship in our lives, we must begin to correct some of the false ideas we've created about worship and begin to embrace the true meaning of worship. Without over-complicating the thought (which I am known for doing); worship restored must involve awe and pleasure.

Returning the Awe to Awesome

Awe is admiration on steroids. To be inclined to worship God, we can't merely be impressed with him; we must be in awe of him. Awe cannot be manufactured; it is a byproduct of experiencing an emotional connection with something or someone as a result of their status, power, or capabilities. Habakkuk 3:2 says, *"I have heard of your fame; I stand in awe of your deeds, LORD."* Many today have not heard or seen enough of God to be impressed, let alone in awe.

A friend of mine once took his son to an NBA basketball game, and sitting a few rows down from them was Michael Jordan. He told his son with excitement to look down there and see. He son was not impressed, as he just saw a guy sitting there—nothing special. His dad told him it was Michael Jordan, and he lit up with excitement and awe. The son said to his dad, "I can't believe it; it's Michael Jordan, the guy from *Space Jam*!" Think about that; not because of his NBA titles, his being arguably the greatest NBA player ever, not even because of his world-renowned Air Jordan Nike shoes; no, his son was in awe because he was MJ from *Space Jam*. He son was in awe, but not for the same reason his dad was in awe. They both were in awe of Michael Jordan because of what they had individually heard and seen from him.

What have today's believers heard about and seen from God to be in awe of him? I believe the better question is this: are believers today devoting enough attention to God in order for them to develop a sense of awe for who he is and what he can do? There are some in the world today who are not impressed with Michael Jordan—not because he's unimpressive, but because they just don't know enough about who he is and what he has done to be that impressed. In the same way, if you want to be in awe of God, you have to devote more time to him than you do to the other things you are impressed with in your life. This is the only way that ignorance becomes feeling impressed, feeling impressed becomes admiration, and admiration becomes awe. To go from ignorance to awe requires attention.

Returning to Our Seats

To restore worship to its rightful owner (God), we as people must return to our rightful places. To return to our rightful places as worshipers and not objects of worship, we must remain in our humanity. Arguably the greatest human spiritual leader, the apostle Paul, said it best: "I am only human." Even the angels who were made greater than us recognize they are only servants, just like us. Not only do we need to put ourselves in our rightful places, we must place other people and things of status in their rightful places in our lives as well. As people, we must always be worshipers of God only. Worship is the highest act of praise, admiration, love, and devotion. It is thus meant only for that which is worthy of all praise, admiration, love, and devotion. No object or person created is worthy of more devotion than the one who created it. Since God is the creator of all things, no person or thing is worthy of having more of our admiration, love, praise, or devotion.

To remain human and to remember we are servants are, in my opinion, the most important parts of restoring worship. Humans in our rightful place are in awe of God by default. Even when God chooses to use us for his great works, we see ourselves as merely servants who take pleasure in being in a high-low relationship with God.

The Pleasure of Worship

Back to sacrifice. Today when we think of sacrifice in worship, we think pain, not pleasure; we think obligation and not privilege. At its core offering, a sacrifice in worship was a sense of privilege. It was a way to engage in the worship relationship that says, "I am yours, and I give out of the pleasure I get from being yours." Imagine that your greatest sport, movie, music, or world hero called you on the phone and asked if you would be willing to do something for them to help champion their cause. Assuming the request isn't illegal, most of us would not respond back by saying our schedules are full, that we've just got off work, that we're too tired, or even simply no thanks. No, we would be doing everything we could to adjust our schedules and disrupt our lives to accommodate their request.

It would not matter how unexpected or how insignificant the request was; we would feel it was a privilege to even be considered to be a part of what they were doing. This is the pleasure of worship. So when Paul says in Romans 12:1 to *"offer your bodies as a living sacrifice, holy and pleasing to God—this is your true and proper worship,"* he's not describing a life of hard living, but a life of pleasurable and privileged living before God. When we offer or submit ourselves in a worship relationship with God, it should not be a struggle for us to do so. In fact, it should be quite the opposite. True and proper worship means it should be a struggle *not* to do so! Worship is not just being obedient; it is not simply being willing. It is offering all of us out of the privilege of being in a relationship with someone we are in total awe of.

The People of Worship

Churches today struggle with their worship gatherings because they struggle with the purpose of their gatherings. In 1 Corinthians 14, Paul shares that the primary purpose of the gathering of believers was to edify and build up the church, which is the gathered believers. So their corporate worship was catered to worshipers, not non-worshipers. A worship gathering is only a worship gathering if those who gather are worshipers of God. Today we have changed the focus of our gatherings to be the place where we bring non-worshipers to become impressed with God so that they may by chance become worshipers of God. This does not match Paul's description of the gathering. The gathering was not where non-worshipers came to be impressed with God; it was where worshipers who were already impressed with God came to gather.

Church gatherings by default should already be impressive because those who are gathering should already be impressed—with God. It therefore should not matter if the gathering takes place in a field, a hole in the wall, a middle school cafeteria, or a cathedral; the level of being impressed should already be sky high. What we should see is individual worshipers gathering together to create a collective worship atmosphere. Instead we see gatherings that cater more to turning non-worshipers into regular attendees or church gatherings that focus on how they can be more attractive to get more people in the seats. To restore worship to our gatherings, we have to make them about God again. We also have to remember that worship is what we do if worshipers are who we are. When we gather together as believers; we must remember that worship is not *for* us, worship is *from* us; to God.

The Place of Worship

Jesus' dialogue with the Samaritan woman in John 4 gives us tremendous insight into the actual location of true worship. The woman asked Jesus which place was the proper place of worship for God's people—on the mountain they stood on or in Jerusalem. In so many words, Jesus told the woman that neither place would be the proper place for worship! He went on to explain why both places were wrong. Jesus tells her that God is spirit, so in order to have a worship relationship with God, one must enter into a relationship that is spiritual or of the spirit realm. A worshiper of God must worship in the spirit. Understood in context, Jesus is saying that true worship doesn't take place in the physical realm because that is not where God resides; true worship must take place in the realm of the spirit.

In the spiritual realm, the physical place of worship becomes irrelevant in many ways. Jesus tells the woman that God is looking for true worshipers who understand where true worship takes place. I can personally say that this has been a humbling discovery for me. God has revealed to me that my worship has depended more on the place than on his presence. Often we are looking for his spiritual presence to enter into our physical world. Oftentimes we are doing external things to create a "presence of God" in the atmosphere. However, I believe it is on us as worshipers to enter into the spiritual realm inside of us, where the Holy Spirit resides, to engage in spiritual worship. This will be our focus moving forward as a family and as a ministry: to learn to enter into the presence of God in the spiritual realm and worship him.

Where is your worship today? Do you sing songs of praise to God because it is part of your obligation or because you are addictively obsessed with him and are floored that someone way out of your league actually cares about you? Today more than ever, we have to break off our worship relationships with anyone or anything who is not God. We must turn our attention and affection solely upon him and allow ourselves to begin to take in his status as the King of kings and Lord of lords, his power as the origin of power itself, and his deeds as the creator of existence.

Everything that we are impressed with should increase our awe of God, because it is he who created all things. We have to stop worshiping the created (idols) and return back to the creator (God) if we wish to restore our true connection with God. At the end of the day, it all comes down to worship. If you desire to follow God with all your heart, mind, soul, and strength, then seek to know him at the level it takes to begin to worship him. Our behaviors, beliefs, and life choices come down to who we are looking up to—if it's not God, then who is it? When faced with the choice of worshiping anything or anyone except God, our choice should be none of the above. Or better put, none above thee.

About Tommy

Tommy Shavers is a speaker, author, minister, and former Christian radio show host. He is president and co-founder of *Unus Solutions, Inc.* and *Tommy Speak LLC.* Tommy is also a contributing author for Linked2Leadership, one of the nation's top leadership blogs. He is a former athlete, teacher, and coach. He holds a bachelor's in Organizational Communication, a master's in both Interpersonal Communication and Biblical Studies, and a Doctorate of Management in Organizational Leadership. Tommy is a USA Track & Field Level 1 Certified Coach and a member of the National Speakers Association (NSA). He has a passion for leadership and personal development and loves to see people work together to make a greater difference in the world.

Other books by Tommy:

The Next CEO: A Leadership Parable (2013)
Life in the Trenches: Joys and Challenges of Christians in Sports (2004 & 2011)

Dr. Tommy Shavers
www.unussolutions.com
www.trueriverministries.com
www.tommyspeak.com

Made in the USA
Charleston, SC
09 June 2014